W9-CGZ-588

Interactive Animal Kit

BEARS

Developed in Cooperation with the Great Bear Foundation

by Robin Bernard

DEDICATION

In memory of JL, a most extraordinary bear.

ACKNOWLEDGMENTS

My thanks to Matt Reid, Director of the Great Bear Foundation, and Dr. Carl D. Esbjornson, member and staff volunteer, for sharing their knowledge of bears with patience and clarity; and once again to my editor, Liza Charlesworth, who makes every project a pleasure.

Cover design by Jaime Lucero and Vincent Ceci
Interior design by JoAnn Rosiello
Book ISBN: 0-590-10106-4

Illustrations by Ivy Rutzky, James Hale, and Michelle Hill
Photo research by Cheryl Moch; Cover photo credit: © Michio Hoshino/Minden Pictures

SCHOLASTIC
PROFESSIONAL BOOKS

New York • Toronto • London • Auckland • Sydney

CONTENTS

How to Use This Book

Welcome to Bears! This unique kit, which includes information, activities, two full-color posters, and an audio cassette, was created to make learning about bears a fun and meaningful experience for you and your students. There's no right or wrong way to use it—feel free to do some of the activities individually or all of them in sequence as a bear unit. Here are a few helpful hints you might find useful in getting the most out of this resource for your class.

1 Invite students to help design your bear theme unit. Find out what your students *really* want to know about bears by creating a KWL (Know–Want to Know-Learned) chart. You may discover that why some bears sleep all winter is more interesting to your students than the scientific classification of the panda. It's important to know students' interests. By having students participate in planning their theme unit you'll be able to focus on what motivates them and they'll feel involved from the beginning.

2 Choose activities that fit the content areas you wish to teach and your students' interests. You don't have to do all the activities in this book. We suggest that you browse through the activities and select those that will connect with your students' interests and learning styles as well as the content areas you want to teach. Feel free to skip from activity to activity as it suits your needs. Be encouraged to adapt, amend, or develop spin-off projects to best meet the needs of your students' levels, attention spans, and preferences.

3 Trade books are a great way to enrich your bear theme unit. Try to assemble a classroom library of both fiction and nonfiction titles about bears that span the reading levels of your students. School librarians, parents, or the students themselves are all great sources for books. We've included a few book reviews throughout this book called **Book Breaks**. There's a complete book list on page 33. Make sure to allow reading time during your bear theme unit so kids can take advantage of the books you've assembled. Children always love having a story read to them so be sure to include this activity.

4 Enrich learning with the companion audio cassette and teaching posters. The audio cassette included in this kit features an interview with bear scientist Matt Reid, along with real bears sounds, an original poem, and a song. Share this tape with your whole class and/or place it in a Bear Learning Center for children to enjoy independently. (Look for the audio cassette icon on the contents page; it tells which components can be found on tape.) And don't forget your two full-color posters! Invite kids to sit around you in a circle as you introduce them to eight exciting bear species, then spend some quality time with the polar bear. (Note: *The Bears of the World* poster is also used with the activities on page 13.)

5 Celebrate bears during the theme unit. Honor and reinforce what the children are learning about bears by displaying their work as well as pictures and newspaper clippings about bears on bulletin boards, in hallways, and on discovery tables. Involve students further by inviting them to make a mural of all the different kinds of bears in their habitats. If you like, invite them to make honey treats or organize a bake sale to help endangered bears.

Bear Hugs

Was there ever an animal that received such ongoing good press? Our warm feelings about bears may have started with a cuddly teddy that shared our crib. Stories about bears were part of our childhoods—from the three bears that found Goldilocks in their house to the adventures of Paddington and Winnie the Pooh—but the wide appeal of bears reaches far beyond storybooks. Viewed as icons of furry virtue and power, they've been adopted as national and state symbols, adorn family crests and dozens of postage stamps worldwide, and are commonly used as environmental logos. The word *bear* has found its way into the stock market, botany (bear's wort, bearberry, bear cabbage) and literally hundreds of athletic teams. Bears not only populate myths, folk tales, and nursery stories, but festivals celebrating them are held in Singapore, Japan, Bolivia, Poland, France, as well as in our own country. When we star-gaze we see sparkling bears that form the Big and Little Dippers—Ursa Major and Ursa Minor.

This book offers your students the opportunity to learn about one of their favorite animals through a wide assortment of fun activities full of fascinating information just waiting to be discovered.

More About Bears

Bears, along with lions, wolves, otters, and other flesh eaters, are in the scientific order *carnivora*. Although carnivores have physical equipment to catch and eat prey, their habitat and particular niche within the carnivora category may affect their diets. When carnivores eat plant matter as well as meat, they're known as *omnivores*. Bears are the largest land-dwelling omnivores of all. They evolved from a small tree-climbing meat-eater and they still have the gut of a carnivore. But a bear's diet (with the exception of the polar and sloth bear's) is about 75 percent vegetation. To get enough nutrition from plant matter, they need to eat a lot of it, so a bear spends most of its time foraging for food.

Pigeon-toed and flatfooted, bears walk in a kind of rolling four-footed shuffle. Their odd gait and plump bodies make them appear clumsy. But they actually are very quick and agile animals and can reach a speed of 40 miles per hour! Most bears can climb and swim, but some species are far better at these activities than others.

The Bear Truth

It's comforting to know that bear attacks on humans are rare. They are, after all, very large and powerful animals, equipped with teeth and claws that can inflict serious harm. Unfortunate incidents can occur if people misled by a bear's cuddly and comical appearance, imagine that it's "tame." Even very small wild creatures may behave with ferocity if they sense danger. Since most of us can't anticipate what might make a bear feel threatened, it's wise to avoid direct contact with them.

TEN BARE FACTS ABOUT BEARS

1. There are eight different kinds, or species, of bears.
2. Minimum weight is less than 100 lbs.
3. Maximum weight is usually about 2000 lbs; the heaviest bear on record weighed over 2500 lbs.!
4. Bears eat both meat and plants.
5. Their front legs are shorter than their hind legs.
6. Bears have 42 teeth.
7. Their curved claws are super strong.
8. Bears walk flat-footed.
9. They have short stubby tails.
10. A bear's sense of smell is superb.

As your students discover more about the abilities, strengths, and intelligence of real bears, respect and caution can be added to the affection they feel for these fascinating animals.

When a bear stands upright it may be looking around, but it's really "smelling" around. People used to consider bears quite near-sighted, but their vision has since been proven to be as good as that of humans. Still, bears are like most mammals who eat meat—they "think" with their noses, relying on their keen sense of smell to find food, a mate, and to spot trouble. Native American lore describes it this way: "If a single pine needle drops to the forest floor, the eagle sees it, the deer hears it, and the bear smells it."

 **BEAR FACT** *A bear's paw prints look very much like human footprints.*

The Who's Who of Bears
There are eight *species*, or kinds, of bears that live on five continents around the world. The different kinds of bears vary in sizes, colors, habitats and diets. But their general body shape is easily recognized as "bear."

American Black Bears
These are our native bears, the clowns and favorites of our national parks. American black bears are the most widespread (and the smallest) bear species on our continent.

Black Bear

In most of the country they have black fur and a brown snout, but in the west they have several color phases that are distinctly different and often confusing. In Alaska and the Yukon, there is a bluish-gray *Glacier* phase. West of the Rockies, some black bears are *Cinnamon*. In British Columbia there is even a creamy white American black bear, known as the *Spirit* or *Kermode* bear.

 **BEAR FACT** *American black bears are the most numerous of all bears.*

Brown Bears
Native to North America, Europe, and Asia, brown bears live in temperate climates. They have a distinctive hump of fat and muscle

Brown Bear

between their shoulders. These are large powerful bears. The world's largest land carnivore is a brown bear subspecies, the *Kodiak* bear. When it stands on its hind legs it can be ten feet tall. It lives on the Kodiak peninsula in Alaska. Another North American subspecies of brown bear is the *Grizzly* bear. Grizzlies are brown with silver tipped hairs. They once roamed every western state. Today only a few grizzlies are found outside of Canada and Alaska, in northwestern national parks. A Eurasian subspecies of brown bear is the *Kamchatkan* bear, which can be nearly as large as a Kodiak bear.

Polar Bears

These ice bears of the Arctic are the most carnivorous of all the species, eating seals, walruses, and dead animals. (Their leftovers often become meals for Arctic foxes and gulls.) With their heavy coats and layers of fat, polar bears sometimes become too hot and will jump into the sea or eat snow to cool themselves. They have the largest feet, are the strongest swimmers, and are the greatest wanderers, although sometimes they find an easier way to hunt migrating seals—they catch rides on sheets of ice. Polar bears, along with Kodiaks, are the largest land carnivores.

Polar Bear

BEAR FACT *In Scandinavian countries, the polar bear is called "ice bear."*

Asiatic Black Bears

These east Asian bears have a thick ruff of fur around their necks and a distinctive white crescent on their chests which accounts for the nickname, *moon bear*. Highly intelligent and temperamental, these bears spend most of their time in trees, avoiding humans and other predators. But neither their intelligence nor arboreal habits have saved them from greedy poachers. Their gallbladders and claws are so highly valued as Asian medical ingredients that the species continues to be hunted relentlessly.

Asiatic Black Bear

Sloth Bears

These shaggy bears are black with white chest markings and live in India, Sri Lanka, and Nepal. Their unique facial structure allows them to feed almost exclusively on ants and termites. They have a two-tooth gap, and a long lower lip which forms a kind of vacuum that noisily sucks up insects. People once thought they were large tree sloths. A cub rides on its mom's back as she moves around and continues to get carried piggy-back style until it's a third her size.

Sloth Bear

BEAR FACT *When sloth bears were first discovered they were believed to be a kind of tree sloth, because they were hanging upside down in trees.*

Spectacled Bear

Sun Bears

Found in Asian tropical forests and called *dog bears*, these are the smallest and least understood of all bear species. But watch out, they have a reputation as one of the most dangerous animals a human can meet in the jungle. Scientists believe sun bears feed on honey, termites, and fruit. But because they're so rare and elusive, they haven't been studied extensively. They're endangered due to widespread poaching and loss of their forest habitat.

Giant Pandas

The most easily identified of all bears, these residents of Asian bamboo forests are a critically endangered species. There are only about 1000 wild pandas left because nearly all of their habitat has been destroyed. Making matters worse is their extremely slow reproductive rate and highly specialized diet of bamboo. A panda must spend about fourteen hours each day eating just to sustain itself. In that time it may consume 50 to 80 pounds of bamboo.

Sun Bear

Spectacled Bears

These are the only bears that live in South America. Gold colored rings around their eyes have given them their name. Living in the remote forests of the Andes, they make "daybeds" in fruit trees, bending branches under them to form a nest, and then stripping off the fruit. These shy vegetarians can also eat and digest plants like cacti, that are too tough for other animals.

Giant Panda

BEAR FACT *A newborn panda weighs the same as a kitten—about four ounces. It develops so slowly that even when it's four months old, it still can't walk!*

Black Bear? Brown Bear?

Color can lead to confusion. Since black bears aren't always black and brown bears aren't always brown, how can a novice bear watcher tell them apart? One way is by size—but that would only work in the unlikely event that both kinds stood side by side! A brown bear is considerably larger than a black one, but the easiest visual give-away is its massive shoulder hump of muscle and fat. Brown bears have longer claws too, and "dished-in" profiles compared to the straighter snouts of black bears.

 BEAR FACTS
Brown bears generally have light colored claws, and black bears have very dark claws.

The claws of a brown bear can be 5 inches long!

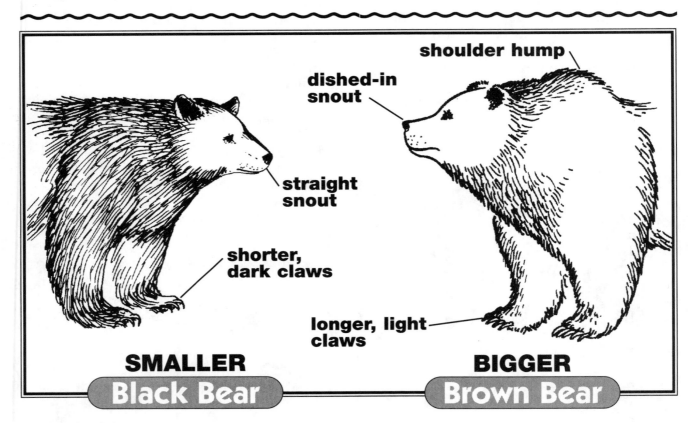

shoulder hump

dished-in snout

straight snout

shorter, dark claws

longer, light claws

SMALLER
Black Bear

BIGGER
Brown Bear

Are Bears Sociable?

Some large mammals live in groups of related individuals (like lions, dolphins, and elephants) and share territory. Not so with any kind of bear. Adults don't get along with each other and usually only meet during breeding season. Many bears may gather in a specific place when food is plentiful, such as a salmon run, but they usually make an effort to maintain enough distance to avoid confrontation.

BOOK BREAK

The Bear that Heard Crying by Natalie Kinsey-Warnock and Helen Kinsey (Cobblehill, 1993) is a retelling of the true story of a toddler who in 1783 became lost in the woods and was protected by a bear until her rescue four days later. The book's illustrations portray the pioneer lifestyle. After students have read the story, challenge them to find examples in the book about how life was different then from today.

Bringing Up Baby

The closest bear relationship is between a female and her cubs. In the middle of winter a hibernating female, half-asleep in her den, may give birth to a litter of two to four cubs. The nearly hairless newborns are toothless, blind, and demanding! Snuggled against their mother for warmth, they nurse noisily on her fat-rich milk. Four or five weeks pass before they have fur and fully opened eyes. When they're about two months old, their mother leads them out of the den. At first they trail after her on wobbly legs, but before long they're chasing, tumbling, exploring, and climbing trees.

Because they have so many skills to learn, bear cubs stay with their mother for a long time—from one to three years, depending on the species. Once in a while a female will adopt orphaned cubs. She is extremely protective, affectionate, and a thorough instructor (which is one reason she doesn't have cubs every year). A mother bear teaches her cubs which plants to eat, how to fish, dig, find honey, and catch insects and small mammals. She also lets them know which animals to avoid, such as porcupines, skunks, and humans. And when the cubs misbehave, she even spanks them! After the second or third winter the female usually sends the cubs off to fend for themselves; the exiled siblings may stay with one another for another two years.

 **BEAR FACT** *A newborn grizzly cub weighs less than a pound.*

Are Bears Intelligent?
The curiosity, learning ability, reasoning, excellent memory, and tool-using skills of bears convince even the most skeptical that bears are extremely intelligent animals. Some biologists think they're as smart as monkeys and apes.

 BEAR FACT *Asiatic black bears have outstanding learning abilities.*

Sleepyheads
Biologists have recently started calling the bears' winter resting period *denning*, because it's quite different from the deep torpor of hibernating ground squirrels and bats. A bear's temperature drops about 12 degrees, and its heart rate slows, but not dramatically, so it's quite easy to awaken. Yet a denning bear isn't totally awake either: It doesn't eat, urinate, or defecate during this period. It survives by burning calories stored in body fat. American black bears and brown bears (both American and European) are the winter sleepyheads. They're the ones that snooze in their dens when food sources have dwindled and deep snow makes movement difficult. To get ready for denning, bears eat practically non-stop throughout the summer and early fall, putting on as much fat as they can. (Black bears can gain 30 pounds a week!) In late summer they chose a den site. It may be under a brush pile, in a hollow tree, or under a fallen log. Black bears often dig out a space among the roots of a large tree, and grizzlies may tunnel into a hillside, using their immense claws to dig out dirt and stones. The bears prepare their hide-aways with a lining of evergreen branches and grass. By late October or early November they enter the dens and begin a sleep that lasts four to seven months.

Copyright © Jerry Lesser, 1996

 **BEAR FACT** *The scientific name for the brown bear is Ursus arctos, which means "bear bear."*

Wide-awake in Winter

As cold as the Arctic is, only pregnant polar bears den. The others continue eating everything they can catch. As for Asiatic black bears, only those living in the northern part of their range are known to use winter denning sites. American black bears that live in the warm southern states also may not den. Sun bears, sloth bears, and giant pandas don't den or hibernate at all.

Once Upon a Time

Fossils found in many parts of the world tell us that bears lived in caves at the same time humans did. The cave bear was a giant—bigger than any bear living today. Stone Age humans hunted them, used their skin for clothing, and their bones for tools and weapons. Although some Native American tribes hunted bears, many others revered them as gods. But when European settlers arrived in North America, bears were shot and trapped by the hundreds of thousands. And inevitably, as people tamed the land, bear habitats vanished beneath cornfields and cement.

BOOK BREAK

Wildlife at Risk: Bears by Malcolm Penny (Bookwright, 1991) explains where bears live, why they are becoming endangered and what is being done to help them. Assign student groups continents and challenge them to come up with a list of endangered bears in their part of the world. The map on the book's page 4 is very helpful.

Omnivore vs. Omnivore

Because of their size and strength, the only serious enemies bears have are also omnivorous mammals—humans. In North America hunting bears for their meat or fur is pretty much a thing of the past, but not so in Asia, where bear poaching is big business. Although synthetic bile is available at a fraction of the cost, real bile (used as medicine) from bear gallbladders continues to fetch high prices. Bears are a symbol of strength, and in Asia, a bowl of bear paw soup sells for as much as $700.

Humans present an even greater danger by destroying habitats. Since even the most powerful animals are helpless against land development and farming, three quarters of all bear habitat has already been lost. Nearly every species of bear is endangered. The up-side is that it may not be too late to help some bears come back from the brink of extinction as we did with polar bears in the 1970s. (The International Agreement on the Conservation of Polar Bears signed in 1973 by five Arctic countries—including

Image provided by IMAGE CLUB GRAPHICS

the United States—protects polar bear populations.) In the last two decades environmental groups have grown in numbers and in political clout. Conservationists now have allies in the media, government, business, and education. Your students can find out more about bear conservation, and how they can help, by writing to:

- ◆ **Great Bear Foundation**
  P.O. Box 2699
  Missoula, MT 59806

- ◆ **North American Bear Society**
  P.O. Box 9281
  Scottsdale, AZ 85252

- ◆ **Wildlife Conservation International**
  New York Zoological Soc.
  185th St. & South Blvd., Building A
  Bronx, NY 10460

Student Activities

Interview with Bear Scientist, Matt Reid (Science) 📼

Invite students to "meet" Matt Reid, the director of the Great Bear Foundation in Bozeman, Montana, *and* a leading bear researcher. On the enclosed audio cassette, Matt answers kids' big questions about bears and talks about his job. Note: After you've enjoyed the Q. and A., stay tuned for the real bear sounds that follow it!

Polar Bear Poems (Language Arts)

The polar bear is one of the most easily recognized and interesting kind of bear. The poster enclosed will give your students an inspiring close-up view at this amazing Arctic hunter. Read the poem aloud to the class and identify all the names that people around the world have for polar bears. Open a general discussion on what the children already know about polar bears and work in some of the additional facts listed here. Then challenge the students to write their own poems about polar bears.

Fun Polar Bear Facts

◆ Polar bears often swim great distances from land while hunting. They use their webbed front feet as paddles, and steer with their back feet.

◆ A Polar bear cub rides on its mom's back in the water, or just hangs onto her tail.

◆ The bottoms of polar bears feet are covered with fur to give them traction on ice and snow.

◆ Of all the bears, polar bears have the best eyesight, and the best sense of smell.

◆ Polar bears—especially cubs—like to play! They slide down snowhills on their bellies, make and play with snowballs, and turn somersaults.

Keeping Warm (Science)

Polar bears are white to blend in with their icy environment—easier to sneak up on prey that way. But under all that fur is black skin, which like all dark colors, soaks up heat. While polar bear hairs may look white, they're actually clear hollow tubes. Like glass, they reflect sunlight down to the bear's dark skin where the heat can be absorbed. Besides reflecting sunlight to the skin, the hollow tubes of hair have air inside them. That trapped air is a barrier between the bears' body heat and the outside cold— insulation. Allow your students to find out for themselves how trapped air blocks cold in the following activity:

1. Fill two small plastic zip-lock bags with ice cubes.

2. Blow air into a third bag and zip it closed. A fourth bag should be left unzipped.

3. Have the children take turns holding their hands out, palms up. Place the air-filled bag on one hand and the unzipped bag on the other.

4. Then put a bag of ice on top of the air-filled bag and on top of the empty bag. Which hand feels colder?

Extension: Have students put a mitten or other woolly thing in the empty bag and try steps 3 and 4 again. *Ask:* Which blocks cold better—air or wool?

BOOK BREAK

The Egyptian Polar Bear *by JoAnn Adinolfi (Houghton Mifflin, 1994) tells the story of a polar bear that becomes the royal playmate of a boy king in ancient Egypt. The author wrote the book after learning that hieroglyphics from an ancient Egyptian tomb recorded plans for a polar bear burial vault. After reading the story aloud to your class, invite them to invent their own story about how a polar bear might have ended up in Egypt.*

Bear Berries (Critical Thinking)

What do American black bears like to eat? Fruits, nuts, seeds, honey, mushrooms, insects, herbs, fish, frogs, meat—and berries! A bear uses its super sense of smell more than any other sense to find its supper. Copy and distribute page 17 to each student and let them help the cub sniff her way through the maze to reach the berries and unscramble the bear foods (Answers: INSECTS, ROOTS, HONEY, FISH, FRUIT.)

Smells to Remember (Critical Thinking, Science)

Because humans rely so much on sight to assess the world around us, we often don't realize how many signals we receive through our noses. Our sense of smell helps us identify things, and particular aromas can trigger vivid memories. Ask the students to give examples of when they "knew" by smell alone that something delicious was cooking, that somebody was burning leaves, or that a skunk was in the yard. Explain that we connect certain smells with particular places, people, and events which help us to remember them. Copy and hand out the reproducible on page 18 to each student. Have the students write down the smells they remember next to the places on the chart. Finish the activity with a class comparison. Did most students remember similar smells for each place?

Extension: Even though bears have a much keener sense of smell than people, your students will be surprised at how many different food smells they can recognize. Set up a "Smelling Station" with different distinct smelling foods—lemons, oranges, chocolate, cheese, peppermint candy, and so forth. Then have student pairs take turns testing each other for the smells. One student is blindfolded while the other holds up the different foods to the blindfolded student. Have them keep track of how many foods they could name—4 out of 6, 5 out of 6, etc.

Three Little Bear Cubs (Music)

Below are words to a song that can be sung to the tune of "Five Little Monkeys." After teaching the song to your students, divide them into small groups. Assign each group a verse number and challenge them to write a verse of their own. You can vary the number of verses (i.e. bear cubs) to fit your class size. The children will enjoy singing their verses to classmates.

First Verse

Three little bear cubs
climbed up in a tree.
One tried to get some honey
and was stung by a bee!

Mama made it better
and she told the bear cub, "See?
That's what you get
for bothering a bee!"

Student Verses

(As many as needed for your class size.)

Final Verse

One little bear cub
climbed up in a tree.
It tried to get some honey
and was stung by a bee!

Mama made it better
and she told the bear cub, "See?
You cannot get the honey
without bothering a bee!"

Where the Bears Are (Social Studies)

North America is home to three species of bear: brown, polar, and black bears. Copy and hand out reproducible page 19 to each student. First have the students cut out the three bear badges. Then ask the children to answer the questions and paste their bear badges in the appropriate circles.

What's in a Name? (Language Arts)

An animal is sometimes named for the person who discovered it, or for the place in which it lives. But very often it's named for the way it looks. Ask the children to carefully examine the *Bears of the World* poster. *Ask:* How do you think the different bears got their names? Do the names fit them? Challenge the students to invent different names for the bears that describe something about them. "Back-pack bears" would be a good name for grizzlies, for example.

Extension: Invite the children to create mythical bears. They can draw them, name them, and share their "discoveries" with their classmates.

Sizing Up Bears (Math)

There's lots of information for students to digest on the *Bears of the World* poster. Comparing the different bear lengths in a graph will make the numbers more meaningful. Each student needs a copy of the reproducible on page 20. Have the students find the length of each kind of bear on the poster and mark it on their chart. Next students can color in the bar for each bear and answer the questions.

Extension: Challenge students to make a similar graph for the different bear weights.

Bear Puppets (Art)

Distribute a copy of reproducible page 21 to each student. Help your students gather the materials, assemble their puppets and learn

to use the "wiggle-tab" to animate them. The bear puppets make a talented cast for the play, "Watching Benny," on page 22. Or you can invite groups of students to create their own bear puppet productions.

You'll Need:

- ◆ heavy paper
- ◆ tape
- ◆ glue
- ◆ craft stick
- ◆ crayons or markers
- ◆ scissors

Share These Directions with Your Students:

1. Reproduce then glue page 21 to a piece of heavy paper.

2. After it's dry, cut out all four parts along the solid lines.

3. Color both bear patterns with crayons or markers.

4. Turn the BEAR PATTERNS over and lay the one with a head on top of the other. To hold the bear patterns together, tape the JOINER as shown in figure A.

5. Next, fold the WIGGLE TAB as shown is figure B.

6. Tape the WIGGLE TAB over the short strip as shown in figure C.

7. Carefully tape the stick to the bottom BEAR PATTERN as shown in figure D.

8. When your puppet is done, wiggle the WIGGLE TAB and watch your bear move its head and legs.

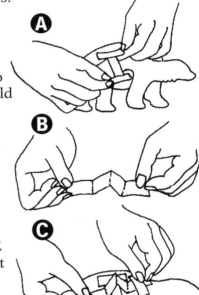

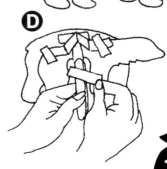

Watching Benny (Drama)

In this short whimsical play, six bears wait for the salmon run to begin. Each bear pretends to be at the river by chance, but when the fish finally appear, all pretense is dropped as they dash into the water after the fish! After first reading the play, the children may enjoy designing and painting a "set" for their puppet performance.

A Tale of a Tail (Language Arts)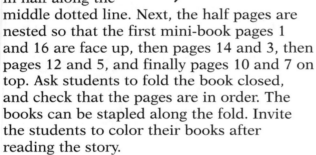

This story is based on a folktale that offers an explanation for the bear's stubby tail, while making a point about bragging. Photocopy reproducible pages 23/24 and 25/26 as double-sided copies and distribute them to your students. Have the children cut the pages in half along the middle dotted line. Next, the half pages are nested so that the first mini-book pages 1 and 16 are face up, then pages 14 and 3, then pages 12 and 5, and finally pages 10 and 7 on top. Ask students to fold the book closed, and check that the pages are in order. The books can be stapled along the fold. Invite the students to color their books after reading the story.

Extension: There are lots of similar folktales and legends about why animals are the way they are: "Why the Raccoon Wears a Mask," "Why a Turtle Has a Shell," for example. Challenge pairs of students to find other such stories in the school library. Then have each student pair "report" on its findings to the rest of the class.

What Bear Cub Saw (Language Arts)

A river attracts a variety of forest animals. It provides food and drink, or a swim. In this poem an American black bear cub describes some of the animals that inhabit his world—including one surprise. Copy the following poem onto chart paper and invite students to read along with the audio cassette.

WHAT BEAR CUB SAW

Walking down by the river
I saw a noisy goose.
Then I saw two beavers there,
and a great big shaggy moose!

I saw an otter splash and dive,
and a badger take a dunk.
Then I saw a fox run from
a pretty spotted skunk.

I saw a bushy-tailed raccoon,
and a bumpy lumpy frog.
I saw a slinky ferret, too,
and some turtles on a log.

Then I looked into the water
which swirled around and around.
But when it grew quite calm again,
do you know what I found?

Right below my very own nose
as clear as it could be—
a furry face with small bright eyes
was looking back at me!

After reading the poem aloud, ask the children what animals the cub saw and list them on the board. Invite groups of students to choose a different kind of bear and come up with a list of animals it might see in a day. (See Who's Who of Bears, pages 5-7.) A polar bear might see seals, Arctic foxes and walruses for instance. Challenge students to find out more about the habitats of their bears, in books. Then have each student group write a new poem about its bear as a cub, including what it saw during a walk. Encourage groups to display the poems or read them to the class.

Extension: Have students draw a panorama of their bear's habitat to accompany their poems. They can include the different kinds of animals, trees, and plants that live there.

Animal Sleepyheads (Science)

Some animals survive the cold foodless winter by simply sleeping through it—*hibernating or denning*. Some animals—like ground hogs, bats, and ground squirrels—enter a deep torpor or true hibernation. Other animals—like raccoons, skunks, and bears—are lighter sleepers that can be awakened by a predator or warm spell. The reproducible pages on 27-28 assemble into a winter scene with fold-up flaps that reveal a critter hibernating in its favorite place, along with a fact about that sleepyhead animal. Photocopy the pages. Then help the children follow the assembly instructions.

Extension: Invite groups of students to delve deeper into the world of hibernation by writing a short report on one of these animals. Each group can share the information about its animal with the rest of the class and all can compare snoozers.

Tipping the Scales (Math)

The average weights of the different bear species can be found on the *Bears of the World* poster. Ask the children to guess what the following animals weigh, and then write the actual weights on the board. Draw a balance scale, and over one side, write "lion" and its weight. Ask the children how many sloth bears would balance the scale? How many polar bears would balance one giraffe? How many pandas would balance a gorilla? How many sun bears would balance a polar bear? How many students would balance a grizzly?

lion: 400 lbs.	dolphin: 350 lbs
giraffe: 2400 lbs.	zebra: 650 lbs.
gorilla: 400 lbs	kangaroo: 200 lbs

Astrobears (Science)

Two of the most familiar constellations—the Little and Big Dippers—are also called Little and Big Bear (Ursa Minor and Major). This activity allows students to identify the constellations and learn something about the folklore behind them. Make double-sided copies of reproducible pages 29-30 and hand one out to each student. (Check that the stars and the bear outline fit together by holding the papers up to the light.) After the students have had their curiosity piqued, invite them to read the explanations on the back about how the bears came to live in the night sky. Have them write their own stories about how they think the bears arrived in the night sky.

Extension: Encourage your students to look for the Big Dipper in the night sky. Drawing its current orientation on the board or providing it on a take-home photocopy with help them locate it. (The Big Dipper is vertical with the "handle" down in winter; horizontal and upside down in spring; vertical with the "handle" up in summer; and horizontal and right side up in autumn.)

Big Bear News (Language Arts)

Extra! Extra! Reproducible pages 31-32 are a fun-to-read newspaper full of true stories and amazing facts about bears. Here are the answers to the sports section:
BOSTON BRUINS—HOCKEY, CHICAGO CUBS—BASEBALL, CHICAGO BEARS—FOOTBALL, VANCOUVER GRIZZLIES—BASKETBALL; and the puzzle:

```
M Q S L O T H B E A R T
H I B E R N A T I O N B
S I P B L A C K B E A R
C U B S X B M O Y L N U
A E D E N L N D K V C M
V L E Z R G R I Z Z L Y
E T C M H N C A F U A J
B W P F I F A K D O W C
E T A X K P J T A V S Q
A R N G B E R R I E S E
R Z D A G O I D N O I C
G K A M C H A T K A N Q
```

Celebrating Bears (Cross-curricular)

Bear's Day is a holiday—like our Groundhog Day—in Austria, Hungary, and Poland. In April, a Ute Tribal Bear Dance is celebrated in Utah. Washington state celebrates its annual bear festival with crafts, food, music, and parades. And in Colorado, there's a special Teddy Bear Picnic Day where everybody brings their teddy bears to the party!

Mark the end of your bear unit with a celebration that lets your students demonstrate and take pride in all they've learned. Here are some ideas for making it a bear–y good time:

◆ Display the children's bear drawings, projects and puppets.

◆ Invite the students to bring their favorite teddy bear or other stuffed animal to school that day.

◆ Talk about bear festival activities from around the country and world, and consider incorporating some into your own celebration.

◆ Read bear stories, poems, and their issue of *Big Bear News*.

◆ Have students put on the puppet plays they've written.

◆ What's a party without food? Snack time can feature yummy bear favorites, like bear cookies, cake, Gummi Bears, or candy made with honey, nuts, fruits, and berries.

Name _____

Bear Berries

Bears are super good smellers. They can smell food that's miles away. This black bear cub smells yummy wild berries. Can you help her find them? But be sure to choose her path carefully—there are some dangers along the way a bear should avoid!

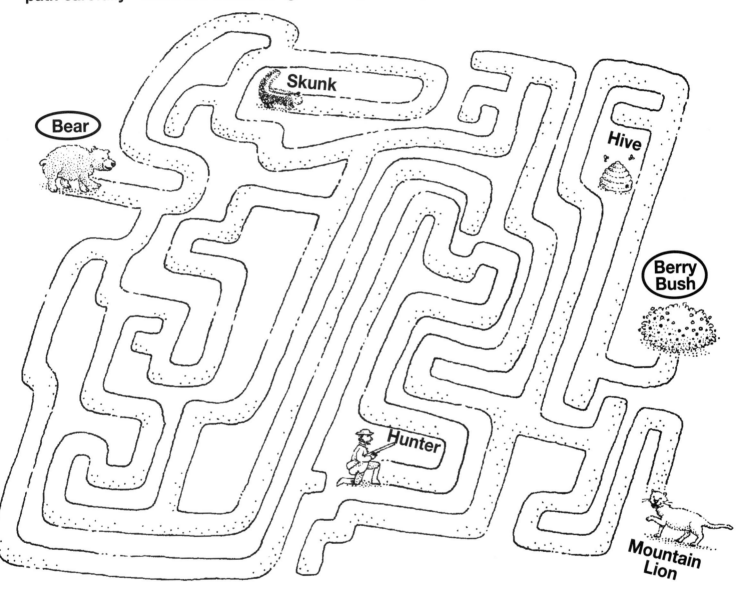

Which path did you choose for this bear? Why?_____

_____

AMAZING EATERS
An American black bear eats just about anything it gets its paws on. Can you unscramble these names of black bear foods?

TNEISCS   SOROT   EYOHN   SFHI   IFTRU

17

Smells to Remember

Bears know lots of smells. They know the smells of their family, and they can smell danger, like smoke or dogs. They know what different foods smell like and can follow the scents to find their lunch.

Your nose knows smells, too! Fill out this chart to find out how many. Just write each smell you remember from each place.

Place	Smells
BAKERY	bread, cookies
CLASSROOM	
GARDEN	
LAUNDRY ROOM	
BEACH	
ZOO	
CIRCUS	
FOREST	
RESTAURANT	
MOVIES	

EXTRA

Which smell-ful place is your favorite? _____

Why? _____

Where Do Bears Live?

Three kinds of bears live in North America—polar bears, black bears, and brown bears. Cut out the three bear badges at the bottom of this paper. Answer the questions below the map. Then use them to tell you where to paste your badges on the map.

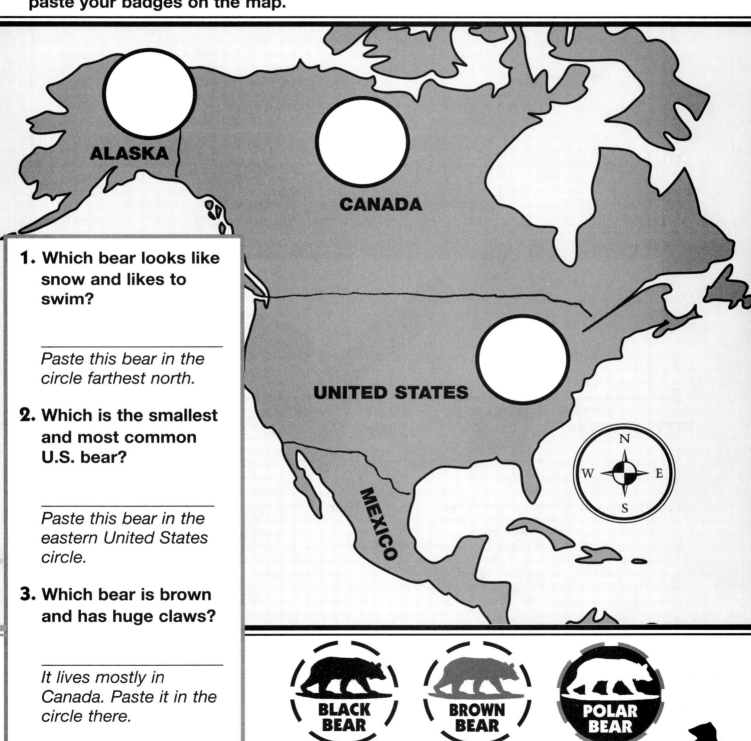

1. Which bear looks like snow and likes to swim?

_____

Paste this bear in the circle farthest north.

2. Which is the smallest and most common U.S. bear?

_____

Paste this bear in the eastern United States circle.

3. Which bear is brown and has huge claws?

_____

It lives mostly in Canada. Paste it in the circle there.

BLACK BEAR

BROWN BEAR

POLAR BEAR

Sizing Up Bears

Find the average length of each kind of bear on the _Bears of the World_ poster. Then color in the bar graph to compare their sizes.

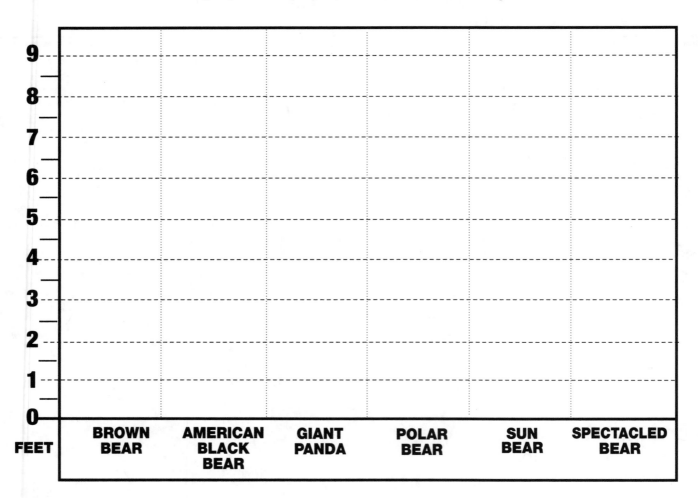

9
8
7
6
5
4
3
2
1
0

FEET | **BROWN BEAR** | **AMERICAN BLACK BEAR** | **GIANT PANDA** | **POLAR BEAR** | **SUN BEAR** | **SPECTACLED BEAR**

1. How many kinds of bears are 6 feet or longer? _____

2. Which is the shortest bear in length?_____

3. Which are the longest bears in length?_____

4. How many kinds of bears are five feet or shorter? _____

EXTRA Get on all fours like a bear. Have a partner measure how long you are

from "snout to tail." Write it here:_____feet _____ inches.

What kind of bear are you closest in length?_____

20

Bear Puppet Pattern

It's "Bear-y" fun to make a bear puppet. Your teacher will tell you how.

WRIGGLE TAB	JOINER

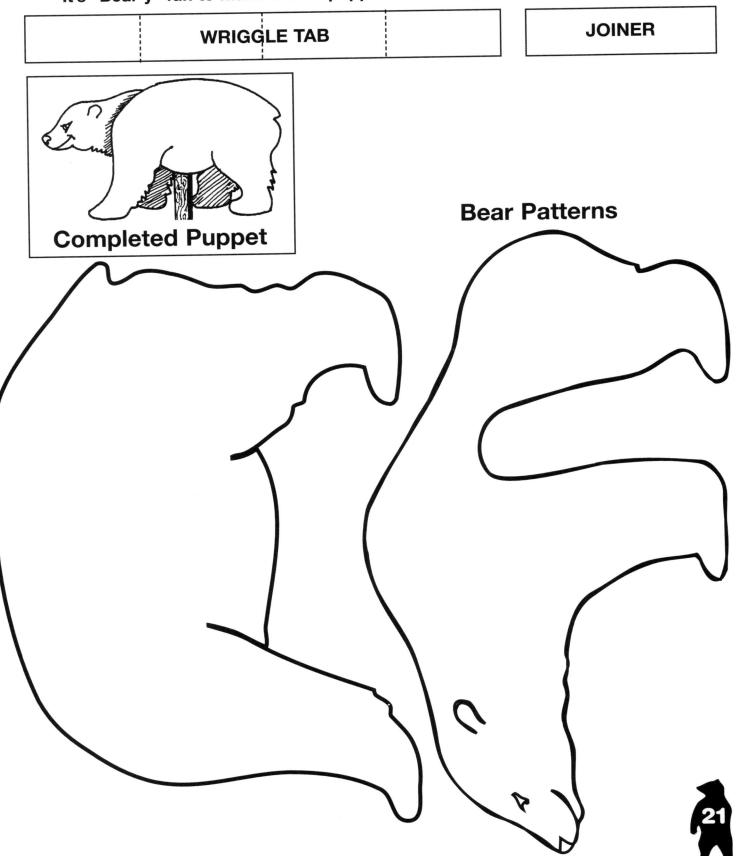

Completed Puppet

Bear Patterns

Watching Benny

BEAR CAST: Benny, Becky, Butch, Bitsy, Borris, and Bella

SCENE: The sun is just rising over a forest clearing by the river bank. It's nearly time for the big salmon run, and as the bears appear, each one pretends to be at the river by chance, hoping the others have forgotten about the fish.

BENNY: *(looking around)* Whew! Nobody's here! Maybe they all forgot the salmon are coming …

BECKY: *(appearing through the bushes)* Good morning, Benny! What brings you to the river so early?

BENNY: *(wading into the water)* Who, me? Oh, my paws are tired, Becky. I think I'll just soak them a while.

BECKY: I see . . .

BUTCH: *(appearing through the bushes)* Good morning, Becky! What brings you to the river so early?

BECKY: Who, me? Oh, I'm just watching Benny soak his tired paws.

BUTCH: I see . . .

BITSY: *(appearing in the clearing)* Good morning, Butch! What brings you to the river so early?

BUTCH: Who, me? Oh, I'm just watching Becky watch Benny soak his tired paws.

BITSY: I see . . .

BORIS: *(appearing from a stand of trees)* Good morning, Bitsy! What brings you to the river so early?

BITSY: Who, me? Oh, I'm just watching Butch watch Becky watch Benny soak his tired paws.

BORIS: I see . . .

BELLA: *(appearing from behind a berry bush)* Good morning, Boris! What brings you to the river so early?

BORIS: Who, me? Oh, I'm just watching Bitsy watch Butch watch Becky watch Benny soak his tired paws.

BELLA: *(passing the others to stand beside Benny in the water)* I see . . . I see . . . I SEE SALMON!

TOGETHER: *(as they all splash into the water)* BREAKFAST TIME!!!

And that's why today Bear only has a tiny stump of a tail, and has never bragged about it again.

6

A Tale of A Tail

Bear tugged and he yanked, he huffed and he puffed, he yowled and he growled, but it wouldn't move.

4

The fur on it was so thick that he spent a long time each day cleaning and combing it.

3

Once, a very long time ago, Bear had a long bushy tail.

2

Finally, Bear took a deep breath and pulled with all his might . . . and SNAP! Bear broke off his tail!

15

Bear thought that his tail was the most beautiful tail of all the creatures in the forest.

4

Before very long, the fish began to nibble, and Bear tried to pull his tail out. But it wouldn't budge! It was frozen fast in the ice!

13

Bear broke a small hole in the ice. Then he sat down and put his tail through it and into the water.

12

One day he met Squirrel in the woods. "What a nice tail you have," he told Squirrel, "but it's not as beautiful as mine."

5

Fox was annoyed with Bear's constant bragging. He said, "Bear, if your tail is so long and wonderful, surely you could use such a magnificent thing to fish with."

10

"What a nice tail you have," he told Raccoon, "but it's not as beautiful as mine."

7

Bear was resting near an oak tree when he met Raccoon.

6

"That's a wonderful idea, Fox," Bear said, and quickly ran off to the frozen lake.

11

Bear was digging in the snow when he met Fox.

8

"What a nice tail you have," he told Fox, "but it's not as beautiful as mine."

9

Animal Sleepyheads

Winter is hard. It's cold. And there's not much food. So some animals just sleep all winter. It's called denning or hibernating.

Here's how to find out who's sleeping where in this snowy scene:

1. First cut along the solid lines. Don't cut on the dotted lines!

2. Then lay this page on top of the one with animals.

3. Now tape or paste the two pages together at the top and along the side.

4. Fold each flap back along the dotted lines to make a window. Now you're ready to sneak a peak at who's hiding underneath!

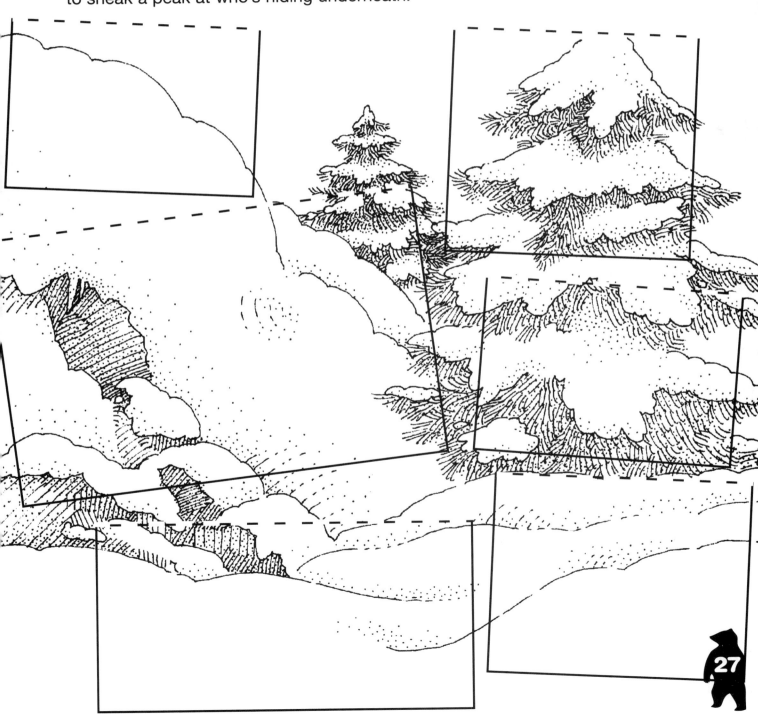

It doesn't wake up until the spring when there are lots of bugs to eat!

Little Brown Bat

This winter snoozer is a light sleeper who wakes up easily.

Grizzly Bear

Even with its thick coat and extra fat, it wakes up very often.

Raccoon

In the northern areas, it's only awake for five months each year!

Ground Squirrel

Ground Hog

During hibernation its temperature drops 50 degrees!

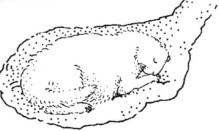

Skunk

This light sleeper usually "borrows" its winter den from another animal.

Astrobears

The Little and Big Dippers are groups of stars. Dippers are old fashioned ladles or big spoons. But these star shapes have other names too. Hold the paper up to the light. You'll see why the Little Dipper is also called Little Bear. And why the Big Dipper is also called Big Bear.

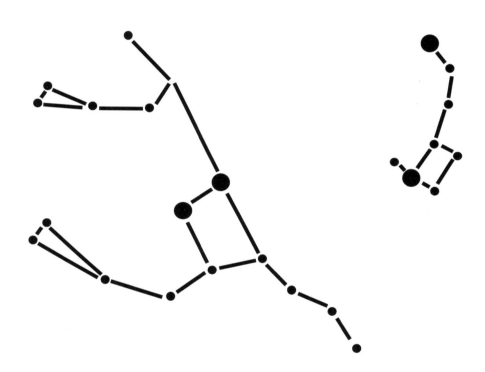

Did You Know?
At the end of the Little Dipper's handle is the North Star. It tells travelers which way is north.

Did You Know?
Did you notice that both bears have long tails? Long ago there were huge cave bears that really did have long tails!

29

How Did the Bears Come to Live in the Night Sky?

◆ **There's an ancient Greek story that says the god Hercules swung the bears by their tails up into the sky for being naughty!**

◆ **A Native American legend says that the animals drew the star pictures in the sky one magical night.**

What do you think? How did these two bears come to live in the night sky? Write your story below.

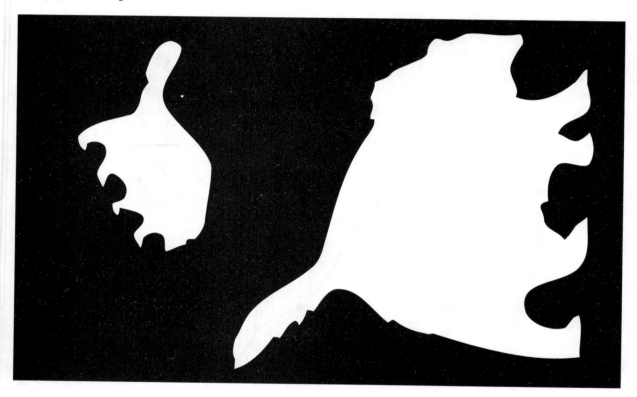

My Starry Bear Tale

_____

_____

_____

_____

_____

BIG BEAR NEWS

Bear Smarts

Gary Alt is a bear scientist. He follows bears to find out how they live, what they eat, and what their dens are like.

One day he was following a bear's paw prints, or *tracks*, in the woods. But all of a sudden the bear tracks just stopped!

There were no rocks for the bear to jump onto. No pond or stream to swim away in. And no trees to climb up. Where could the bear have gone? It was like it just disappeared!

Alt turned around and started following the paw prints back the way he came. He studied those tracks for about fifty yards back. Finally, he noticed that there were toe marks at *both* ends of each print.

The bear had "back-tracked"! It had turned around and walked back the way it came by stepping only in its own tracks.

Even though Alt finally figured out how the bear had fooled him—the bear won. The bear was long gone. Alt never saw it.

SPORTS SCENE

Did you know that lots of sports teams have bear names? Here are a few. Draw a line to match the team name to the sport.

BOSTON BRUINS   **BASEBALL**

CHICAGO CUBS   **BASKETBALL**

CHICAGO BEARS   **HOCKEY**

VANCOUVER GRIZZLIES   **FOOTBALL**

Dining Out

What's a bear's favorite food? Check out these different bear menus. Do any bears eat things that you like to eat?

- The sloth bear loves termites and ants. They have a special long snout and lips that they use like a vacuum to suck up bugs. These noisy eaters can be heard sucking up supper from super far away!

- Spectacled bears like to munch on prickly cactus plants!

- Picky pandas pretty much only eat bamboo shoots and leaves.

- North American brown bears aren't fussy eaters. They eat more than 200 different kinds of plants, plus meat and fish.

- Kamchatkan bears prefer a fishy menu. They eat about 80 pounds of fish a day!

- Polar bears eat only every five days. So when they do eat they eat a lot! One meal might be 150 pounds of seal meat.

Bear Hunt

Find the 12 bearish words below in this puzzle!

```
M Q S L O T H B E A R T
H I B E R N A T I O N B
S I P B L A C K B Y N R
C U B S X B M O Y L A U
A E D E N L N D K V N M
V L E Z R G R I Z Z L Y
E T C M H N C A F U A J
B W P F I F A K D O W C
E T A X K P J T A V S Q
A R N G B E R R I E S Q
R Z D A G O I D N O I C
G K A M C H A T K A N Q
```

HIBERNATION	**PANDA**
KAMCHATKAN	**DEN**
CLAWS	**BLACK BEAR**
CAVE BEAR	**CUBS**
BERRIES	**GRIZZLY**
SLOTH BEAR	**KODIAK**

THE RECORD BOOK

★ A black bear in Pennsylvania weighed more than 800 pounds.

★ The heaviest polar bear weighed 2210 pounds.

★ The heaviest brown bear weighed more than 2500 pounds.

Image provided by IMAGE CLUB GRAPHICS

Cub's Corner

• Grizzly cubs can climb trees. But their parents can't follow because they're too heavy!

• Panda cubs can't walk until they're four months old.

• Newborn bears don't have teeth, can't see or hear, but can make a lot of noise!

• Kodiak cubs double their weight every two months.

• Naughty cubs get spanked by mother bears.

• Polar bear cubs ride on their moms in the water.

• Sloth bear cubs get piggy-back rides while their moms walk, run, and climb trees.

Illustration by Jan Pyk.